LOST QUOTES

BY JOHN MARKS

ILLUSTRATED BY CHRIS BONNO

COVER DESIGNED BY MIKE FLECKENSTEIN

AAron,
Enjoy!

John Marks

HAN HOUSE

Published by
HAN HOUSE PUBLISHING
Huntingdon Valley, PA

Library of Congress Cataloging-in-Publication Data
Marks, John, 1997
Lost Quotes/ by John Marks
ISBN 0-9642648-1-1

Printed in the United States of America

1st Printing, 1994
2nd Printing, 1997

Gilliland Printing, Inc.
Arkansas City, KS

Illustrated by Chris Bonno
Cover designed by Mike Fleckenstein

THE HAN HOUSE STORY

H.A.N. - HELPING AUTHORS AND ARTISTS NOW

Han House Publishing, established recently, is modeled after the attitude the rulers of the Han Dynasty in China had thousands of years ago. The Emperor Han decreed that a stipend be paid to all who wrote and drew. The people created and were paid. Expression and happiness was rampant. Exchange of ideas and art was common and natural. The country flourished. The people loved the Emperor Han. The people were happy. The Emperor was happy. The entire country was happy. Then, at 4:47 PM on a beautiful Tuesday, Mongol hordes came sweeping down from the steppes and ruined everything. Here at Han House Publishing, we promise never to let that happen again.

INTRODUCTION

Throughout history, ancient to recent, many people have been quoted saying all kinds of things. Well, some of those quotes were lost.

I can still remember the thrill of discovering my first Lost Quote. To set the scene: it was a beautiful afternoon in 1986... summer was around the corner and there was a certain excitement in the air. There I was at the Library of Congress, researching for a comedy bit on Columbus, and, having found just about all that I needed to bring my piece to full punch, I was dutifully reshelving Joe Harris' *"History of World Exploration for Dummies"* when two things happened in rapid succession.

First, I flashed back to the previous evening when I had been watching TV and an ad for the Lost Episodes of "The Honeymooners" captured my eye and imagination. The thought of all that footage, brimming with comedic genius, lying dormant in a vault for thirty years just blew my mind.

Then, in the next millisecond, as I reached to replace my massive tome on the top shelf, it slipped from my hand; I fumbled and awkwardly caught the corner of its back cover. The book flung open and, lo and behold, out fluttered a small torn piece of paper etched with worn and faded handwriting, in quotation marks. My initial reaction — that this was some crusty old bookmark, or some college student's crib-sheet, or some other mundane scribbling that I should leave for some government employee to sweep up — quickly dissolved into the background as I revisited Ralph Cramden bellowing "To the moon Alice, to the moon!"

The thought that there might be a connection between Ralph Cramden and Christopher Columbus (other than that they both had a best friend named Norton) had never occurred to me. But there I stood, about to gaze upon words which were probably lost in time, much like those now treasured "Honeymooners" episodes. I felt as if I was on an Apollo mission to the moon (one of the successful ones) and Houston Control had just said "Ignition... Blast off!" I was holding a Lost Quote!

With that revelation simultaneously inspiring and unnerving me, I braced my shaking hands against the bookcase, lowered my gaze, focused, and with a gasp, realized that it was a quote from Christopher Columbus joking around with his crew, as they were sailing to the New World. It said:

"Look! The Edge of the Planet!... Just kiddin'."

You can only imagine my excitement. If this quote had been lost, then there must be others. I looked for more Lost Quotes in the Library of Congress that very day. As I traveled around the country doing stand-up comedy, I did research in libraries, museums, archives, and pool halls. What follows is the result of an arduous and tireless quest to bring to the masses the historical quotes that have been lost. I hope you enjoy Lost Quotes.

John Marks

DEDICATION

To my wife, Joni, and my daughter, Angelica, for giving me love and perspective. To my wonderful friend "Mr. Bonno" for bringing a bunch of these scenes to life. To my buddy Fleck for excellent design ideas. To Kiri's brother Chip for layout and technical support.

AND A SPECIAL THANKS TO

Maury Harris, my writing partner and great friend since I was two years old. You know, not too many people can say that!

NOTE TO READERS

I must warn you that Lost Quotes is a very rich reading. It's like a Whitman's Sampler. You don't want to finish reading it in one sitting, you could get sick; thus, the warning. I'd rather you get a sample taste in the bookstore, carry it around, share with other people, see if you prefer it. Taste again, buy it, take it home, take your time, enjoy it, call your friends, tell them about it, order T-shirts. Then go back to the bookstore and buy the remaining copies as gifts. The point being, don't try to read this whole book while in the bookstore, it's too much, it's dangerous, your head could explode, and I don't want to get that phone call. "Uh, Mr. Marks, we're going to have to return your copies of Lost Quotes. We've had too many customers' heads explode from trying to finish your book in one standing. One guy's last words were, 'But I've only got three pages left!' then, kaboom." Let's face it, here at Han House, we don't need that kind of liability.

©BONNO/MARKS 96

"Look! The Edge of the Planet! . . .
Just kiddin'."

-Columbus to his crew

"After we take Russia, we sell it to China. Then we take China and sell it to Japan. Then we take Japan and sell it to the United States. Then, if we can take the United States.... Do you see where I'm going with this?"

-Napoleon discussing strategy

"I can't believe I forgot my umbrella!

-Noah on the Ark

"I keep seeing Indians."

-Custer's psychic

"Dan, could you please wait outside? I'm talking to the National Security Council."

-President Bush to Quayle

"I'm so tired of this armor. Why don't we try some spandex and padding?"

-*Sir Lancelot*

"Why do you want a sword for Christmas? How about some Barbie Dolls?"

-*Joan of Arc's mother*

"This Iran-Contra thing will fizzle out fast."

-*President Reagan*

I know it's an extra-terrestrial spacecraft. Just shut up!"

-*Buzz Aldrin to Neil Armstrong*
on the moon

"Oh no, one crusade to the Middle East is enough for me!"

-King Richard's neighbor

"So you see, the universal mind of man is... are you people getting this at all?"

-Socrates addressing a crowd

"I can't believe I forgot my raincoat!"

-Noah on the Ark

"...so I took my sword and stabbed him right in the throat. You should have seen the look on his face. More wine for everyone! Then there was the time I..."

-Genghis Khan telling war stories

"I keep seeing snow."

-Napoleon's psychic right before he went into Russia

"So what do philosophers make an hour?"
                                        -Socrates' neighbor

"Honey, he's not a sweet garden snake! He's a serpent!
Why did you invite him to dinner?"
                                        -Adam to Eve

"Some of those peppermint sticks, a few licorice
whips, and a handful of jawbreakers. Hey! Hurry up
before my ice cream melts."
                                *-young Billy the Kid robbing
                                        a drug store*

"Once it's skinned and gutted, you can put a spit right
through it and it will roast up in just a few hours over
hot coals."
                                *-St. Francis of Assisi discussing
                                        his recipe for wild boar*

"Moses, for petesake, it's been forty years, will you please pull over and ask somebody."

-Mrs. Moses

"Wouldn't it suck if this Watergate thing blows up in your face?"

-Spiro Agnew to Nixon

"Now tell me again. Does the sun rise in the east or the west?"

Clark to Lewis on the way to the Pacific Ocean

"Leif, go get your brothers, Stick and Tree, and clean up your room."

-Mrs. Ericsson

"You know, for the life of me, I can't remember which one of these dad-blamed stars we're following."

-One of the three wise men

"Now is the winter of our discontent. But I promise, this spring, we'll have a big white sale!"
                                    -Richard III

"Never jog in wooden shoes!"
                                    -Dutch proverb

"I would say that my secret to longevity is bran."
                                    -Methuselah

"Gee, your office is bigger than mine."
                                    -Dan Quayle to Bush

"Clinton, dude, you're wastin' my pot, man!"

-The guy sitting next to Clinton when he said he smoked pot but didn't inhale

"Curse age! I've been waiting to die for over 300 years now. Today I fell down the stairs and broke my hip for the 12th time. That, along with arthritis, anemia, Alzheimer's, and whatever else, makes old age a living hell. I keep wanting to see a white light but it's not happening. It's sad when you go to your great great great great grandkid's funeral and they lived a full life. I'm one of the few people living who prays to be hit by lightning. It already happened once, in my early 300's, and it didn't kill me. When I go to sleep at night, I hope I don't wake up, or at the very least that my house catches fire in the middle of the night and I'm burned to a crisp like my great great great nephew-in-law did 200 and some odd years ago. He was 270. The weird thing about all this is that up until age 50 I was an optimist. Then I had that dad-gum hatchet accident. My foot has never been the same. The same year, I suffered an aneurysm, two broken legs, a blood clot, two fingers amputated, malignant pancreatic cancer, food poisoning, was mugged twice, almost drowned, my second wife left me, and a pack of wild dogs attacked me on the way home from a mumbelety-peg tournament. So please excuse my pessimism. Yours truly, Methuselah."

-Methuselah at 452 in a letter
to his cousin

"Did you know that if you put an L on the end of NASA, it would spell NASAL?"

-Dan Quayle

"I can't believe I forgot my fishing pole!"

-Noah on the Ark

"Personally, I'd like to paint the White House a nice mauve color!"

-Mrs. Grover Cleveland

"Round? I've always felt that the planet was oblong."

-Columbus' neighbor

"You know we're not the first. Leif Ericsson was here almost 300 years ago."

-*The First Mate to Columbus*

"I shall return..., now do you spell the name of this island with an F or a PH?"

-*MacArthur leaving the Philippines*

"I can't believe I forgot my shaving kit!"

-*Noah on the Ark*

"I keep seeing rope."

-*Mussolini's psychic*

"Let me see. Finish the march to Rome. Destroy the Senate's troops. Get Uncle Leo's prescription filled."

-*Caesar going over his To Do list*

"There's nothing like a cup of coffee and a hit of acid in the morning."

-Timothy Leary

"Okay men, today I want to talk to you about family values."

-Kublai Khan addressing his troops

"Okay men, now that we have Jericho and Gaza, I say we attack."

-Yassir Arafat

"But why me Lord? I am slow of tongue, poor of speech, and my feet are absolutely killing me."

-Moses at the burning bush

"Oh no! The ocean has risen and we can't get back across the Bering Strait."

-An Indian when they tried to go back

"I told him to keep it short."

-Mrs. William Henry Harrison
talking about her husband's
long inaugural speech on a cold
day in Washington D.C., where
he caught pneumonia and died

"Let me see.   Write Mom.   Kill Alexander Hamilton. Plant rosemary and ginger in the garden."

-Aaron Burr going over his
To Do list

"No Mother, I haven't been talking to Allen. I've been talking to Allah, the One Supreme God!"

-Mohammed

"And no, my friends don't call me Genghy!"

-Genghis Khan to his spear captain

"Do you know what I've missed the most since I've been in seclusion? Putt-Putt!"

-Salman Rushdie

"It says in Revelations, chapter... uh, chapter... uh, hey Tony, what chapter was that locust thing?"

-the Pope in 1455 A.D.

"Just my luck! I invent peanut butter, the highest protein, greatest sandwich spread ever, and it sticks to the roof of my mouth."

-George Washington Carver

"Sometimes I think, Joe, you could have been a great dancer."

-Stalin in his later years

"Kill him, kill him, kill him, have lunch with him, kill him."

-Stalin going over his To Do list

"As gifts we brought gold, frankincense, myrrh, and a Tickle-Me Elmo."

-One of the three wise men

"After I finish this flying machine, I have plans for an etch-a-sketch."

-Leonardo Da Vinci

"If I ever have a son, I think I'll name him Chip."

-Michelangelo while working on the statue of David

"Quick! Somebody give me a C!"

-Mozart at a party

"I can't believe I forgot the paddles."

"Pablo, quit distorting your face like that. It will get stuck that way."

-*Picasso's mother*

"How about 'Tootsie Roll' Dole? No. How about 'Big Bowl Headed' Dole? No. How about 'Beat the Poll' Dole? No. How about Bob 'King' Dole, you know, like Nat King Cole? No. How about...."

-*Bob Dole coming up with nicknames for his campaign*

"Sure is quiet out here!"

-*Thoreau at Walden Pond*

"I'm almost finished writing my book and I still can't decide on a name. This is my life's effort and you'd think the title would be flashing in my head like a lighthouse before I started even writing it. Here are my choices. Let me know what you think! "Sittin' Around Walden Pond", "At Walden Pond", "Thoughts from Sitting Next to Water", "Pond Driven Thoughts", "Alone, and I Can't Swim", "I Wish I Had A Fishin' Pole", "The Pond, It Speaks to Me", "If I Could Only Get A Job", "Civil Disobedience and Crickets", "Me, My Shoes, and No Boat", "The Where and Why of Trout Fishing", "Thoreau's Fishin' Tips", "Where's My Hook?", "Dog Paddlin' is All I Need to Know", "Skimming the Bottom", "In Search of Meaning Next to an Ant Bed", "Fishing Tips and How to Fight the Establishment", "All You Need is Solitude, a Typewriter, and a Good Bottle of Whiskey", "I Need Some Company", "The Silence is Deafening", "I think I See Somebody", "I Fear Not the Bogey Man", and "On Walden Pond." Let me know which one you like. Fondest Regards. Henry."

-Henry David Thoreau in a letter to a friend, from Walden Pond

"Of course my ultimate goal is track lighting!"

-Thomas Edison

"Darn it honey, the only clean sheet I have to wear has that Flintstone pattern on it! And just my luck, it's a fitted sheet!"

-Gandhi

"Columbus just found out the Earth isn't flat, it's round. Every single one of those flat globes we made is worthless!"

-Gino Luchese, the largest maker of flat globes in Europe in 1492

"This guy Homer keeps buggin' me for details of our battle with the Phoenicians. I told him I'd contact him when I had time. If he asks me again, I'm going to punch him in the face."

-Greek general

"Columbus, dude . . . those are some fluffy
pants, man!"

-The First Mate

"Sure I'll be blocking back. I'll cut a path! Throw me the ball, I'll catch it! If you want me to pitch it back, I'll do that. You call the plays, I'll execute them. You design the game plan. I'll study the play book. Oh, ... Bob, can I get you more coffee?"

-Jack Kemp to Bob Dole while being considered as a running mate

"The other morning I woke up in my hotel to the sound of gunfire in the room above me. You can imagine my consternation. I pulled out my six shooter, fired through the ceiling, one foot left of the fan and apparently nailed the culprit right through the skull. They say he dropped like a puppet."

-Doc Holliday in a letter

"You know guys, I never really liked Hitler. I was just playing the game, waiting for the right moment to take him out. You know! I was in the process of positioning myself! All I've got to say is, damn that Staffenberg! What do you say you let me go?"

-Field Marshall Wilhelm Keitel's last words before being hung for war crimes in Nuremberg

"Okay men, on the count of three we charge the castle. Now don't forget, there is a moat, so no pushing."

-King Richard before a battle

"I just want to fly around and clear my head a little bit. I won't be long!"

-Rudolph Hess to Hitler before he flew to Scotland during World War II

"Hess went to Scotland! Uh Oh!"

-Hitler

"Well honey, I've narrowed it down to either Deep Throat or Long Esophagus."

-Deep Throat, of Watergate fame,
deciding on his name

"What do you mean you're pregnant?"

-Gregory Pincus, inventor of the
birth control pill, to his wife

"Honey I can't sleep!" I can't seem to get that big jousting match out of my mind."

-Sir Lancelot

"Newt, your cousin Salamander is here to play. Y'all stay outta that creek."

-Mrs. Gingrich to young Newt

"We are now in what I predict will be the future state of Montana as soon as we can bring together a signed contract with the Indians and then break it. I have to be honest, the fresh air is great, the travel is great, the scenic lands are great, the Indians have been quite friendly, but Clark is about to drive me crazy. If I've heard it once, I've heard it a thousand times. 'Are we ever going to get to the Pacific Ocean?.' I may go down in history as the first great explorer to kill his partner in his sleep. If I only knew in St. Louis that he was such a whiner. Here's another line: 'Oh great, more Indians.' Of course there are more Indians, they live here. He's never happy. The campfire smoke bothers him. The fish is never fresh enough. His feet are always tired. When the moon is out, he can't sleep. His pack is always too heavy, and he's constantly saying 'Why can't we meet some Indians that know how to give great foot massages?' Sincerely, Lew."

-Lewis, of Lewis and Clark, in a
letter to his brother

"Man, I'm freezing my butt off!"

**-Rear Admiral Peary going
to the North Pole**

"If you ever run into the Abominable Snowman, don't ask him if he prefers the name 'Yeti'."

-*Chinese proverb*

"Pass the salt, pass the pepper and the cream cheese. Where's my bagel? Oh wait, it's on the spike of my helmet. I'm such a nut!"

-*Kaiser Wilhelm at breakfast*

"Sell Louisiana but keep my apartment on Bourbon Street."

-*Napoleon*

"I don't care what anybody says, no snow ice cream tonight!"

-*Rear Admiral Peary going to the North Pole*

"Anyway, the kingdom of heaven is... somebody give Andrew the Heimlich maneuver. I think he's choking on a bone."

-Peter speaking at a fish fry

"John, I believe you can come up with something better than 'We're not ready to die yet.'"

-John Paul Jones' first mate
helping him with his
famous line

"Well, should we publish Mein Kampf, or my hilarious book of social faux pas?"

-Hitler to his publisher

"A giant white hammer and a popsicle."

-Lenin's first choice for the
Soviet Union's flag

HAMMER & SICKLE
PUBLISHING

"What do you mean you want a chase scene?"

*-Karl Marx talking to his editor
about Das Kapital*

"Hmmm, Romaine lettuce, oil, egg, and anchovies...?"
-Caesar in the kitchen

"Noah, the tigers got loose and ate three species of reptiles, plus they got Billy's leg!"
-Noah's first mate

"Sometimes illiteracy makes me so sick I just want to douse it with gasoline, light it with a match, watch it burn to a crisp, and then tap dance on it like a big toad wearing hiking boots."
-Barbara Bush

"...and I tore cartilage in both of my knees. That same night, while in the middle of REM sleep, I rolled out of bed and broke my collar bone. My great great great great great grandkids heard the noise and thought it was a burglar. The sheer weight of all of them piling on me broke my other collar bone and collapsed my good lung. On the way to the doctor's office our cart rolled off the road 150 feet into a ravine. I suffered severe lacerations and broke both of the arches in my feet. I jumped at the last second. My great great grandson and his wife were knocked unconscious. Sam, as I lay there with lacerations, two broken arches, two broken collar bones, torn cartilage in both knees, and a collapsed lung, I thought to myself, 'Well, Methuselah, you're 610 years old now, maybe it's your time to go.' Sam, I was ready. I could see it. I could smell it. This was the end. Then, a band of thieves came over the hill, about a dozen of them, and stole everything. They broke my ankle pulling off my left shoe. Aaron and Mary came to and carried me to the doctor. That was my weekend."

-Methuselah in a letter

"Hey Columbus! Loan me some money, man! I want to buy some fluffy pants like that!"

-*The First Mate*

"Okay, this is the last time I tell you people. God is in Heaven and the devil is in Hell."

-the Apostle Andrew
addressing a crowd

"I can't believe I forgot my galoshes."

-Noah on the Ark

"Does triangulation mean anything to you?"

-JFK's psychic

"No I haven't taken Britain. Did I say I've taken Britain?"

-Caesar talking to reporters

"I shall defeat you by any means necessary."
-Malcolm X during a high school chess match

"Hillary, I just baked some fresh cookies. Would you like some?"
-Mrs. Rodham to a young Hillary

"He's tall, handsome, and smart, but you could die from his breath."
-Joseph Lister's prom date

"Not red, *per se*, more of a plunder brown with auburn highlights."
-the hairdresser to Eric the Red (formerly Eric the Brown)

"Hey! Leave the dog alone and quit ringing that doorbell!"

-Pavlov's mother ∘

"At last count you have 1,238 animals in your back-yard. I had to send 3 men to Flood Lane because none of them can count over 500. If you want us to even consider the possibility of you keeping all of those animals then they need to get their distemper and rabies shots, plus they need to be spayed or neutered. You keep saying it is going to flood. It hasn't flooded here! Ever! Regards, Animal Control."

-Animal Control in a letter to Noah

"I know you haven't been paid in a while, but I can't believe you ate that raven I sent you."
-Edgar Allen Poe's editor, miffed about his client's missed literary opportunity

"I can't stand him, I tell you! That Atilla the Hun just gets under my skin!"
-an opposing general

"Lions, check. Tigers, check. Emus... Emus? What the hell is an Emu?"
-Noah going over his list

"He'll march to Montgomery but he won't take his dirty clothes to the laundry room."
-Mrs. Martin Luther King, Jr.

"All right, somebody go get two gnats and let's get the hell out of here."

-Noah right before the Ark set sail

"First, you're wrong! The total count of animals I have is 3,047: 678 reptiles, 283 amphibians (I lost a newt), 2,086 insects. (Only 1.4 million left to go. Do you know where I can find an East Asian cockroach?) I've spent most of my time counting, so I know. I should be spending my time building this stupid Ark, it's already started to rain. Billy, you also miss the point. I can't spay and neuter these animals, for they are the ones that will keep their species alive after the flood. Don't you see the synchronicity of me living on Flood Lane? I keep telling everybody and I'll tell you again, God wants me to collect two of every animal, build an Ark (a big boat) and soon it will rain for forty days and forty nights and kill everything but us. I look at it as kind of a heavenly spring cleaning. Anyway, that's it, I have lots to do. Fondest Regards, Noah. P.S. - Do you know where I can get two kangaroos?"

-Noah in a letter to Animal Control

"It's large and it's colorful, and quite frankly, gentlemen, it's the tastiest bird on the continent. I should know. I've eaten every bird on the continent, post haste, and I can assure you that the bald bird of prey doesn't taste any better than your average hoot owl."

-Ben Franklin making his case for the turkey as our national symbol

"Damn! The rattlesnake bit me again! I can't believe I forgot the bandages!"

-Noah on the Ark

"Okay men, whoever builds the biggest snowman in 25 minutes gets an extra blanket tonight."

-Washington at Valley Forge

©BONNO/MARKS 96

"Sure he's a General, but he can help row the boat."

-Two privates talking while Washington was crossing the Potomac

"So this is the Ovaltine Office."

-*Dan Quayle walking into the
Oval Office for the first time*

"I told you I love you. Now I suppose you'll want me to count the ways."

-*Marital spat at the Browning house*

"There's a bunch of them, but I think we'll make it!"

-*Custer at Little Big Horn*

"It's Attila the Hun, not Attila the Fun. I get so sick of having to explain that."

-*Attila the Hun*

"I don't believe the Earth is round or flat! I think it's sort of a misshapen rectangle!"

-Queen Isabella to Columbus

"What do you say we fly out to Wright Patterson Air Force Base, look at the dead alien bodies, and then I'll take you to dinner."

-President Dwight D. Eisenhower to his wife, Mamie

"It's a New World! I see it! We've found a New World! Fourteen months at sea, and we found it! Okay men, enjoy the New World while you can. Tomorrow we set sail for home."

-Leif Ericsson to his men

"I can't seem to get the ketchup out of the bottle."

-Max Planck, 1918 Nobel Prize winner and inventor of Quantum Mechanics

"Yeah, I discovered radioactivity, but now I've got this growth on my arm."

-Antoine Henri Becquerel,
the discoverer of radioactivity
who won a Nobel Prize in 1903

"Damn it! I know that Northwest passage is here somewhere!"

-Henry Hudson the day before his ship's
crewmember's mutinied and put him in an
open boat in the middle of Hudson Bay —
He was never heard from again.

"Never kickbox with a kangaroo."

-*Australian proverb*

"Float like a butterfly! Sting like a mosquito! No. Float like a butterfly! Sting like a yellow jacket! No, that's closer. Float like a raft! Sting like a gnat! Now I'm way off!"

-Muhammed Ali working on his famous line

"Never attack Kuwait twice."

-Iraqi proverb

"You had to go and tell everybody we're not the center of the universe."

-the Copernicuses arriving home
from a party

"Last Thursday had to be the worst day of my 722 years of what is commonly called 'life.' My descendants helped me to the park down the street. On the way, they dropped me twice out of sheer ignorance. They helped me to my favorite park bench and I told them to pick me up in an hour. I told them I've had severe arthritis in both of my legs for 260 years and I don't get around very well. When they left it was sunny and about 80 degrees. Ten minutes later it drops to about 15 degrees, the sky opens up and starts to pour hail the size of my fists. I'm stuck on this park bench getting pummeled. Everyone is scurrying under trees and ignoring me. I thought, 'well, this is it. I can only take so many blows to the head from fist sized hail. My time has come.' Just when I thought it couldn't get any worse, a band of marauders came over the hill, about 50 of them. They were shooting their arrows at everything that moved. People were dropping all around me. I was freezing. I counted 24 blows to the head from fist sized hail. Then I caught an arrow in the shoulder that pinned me to the park bench. As the marauders rode by me I yelled out in my most venomous voice 'You should be ashamed!' Next thing I knew I woke up in the doctor's office."

-**Methuselah in a letter**

"I just received a letter from your mom last week about your plan to fly. The reason I'm writing you is because Wilbur won't listen. When I say to him that man wasn't meant to fly, he doesn't hear me. You do. I talked to Mr. Phelps and he assures me your old job at the drug store was waiting for you. Wilbur on the other hand will have to seek work elsewhere. That formaldehyde incident has forever stained his career. What possessed him to pour formaldehyde into the jelly bean jar? Anyway, this is an appeal to reason. Let birds fly. Let man walk and stock candy shelves. Uncle Reese."

-*Orville Wright's Uncle Reese in a letter to Orville*

"You FORGOT the peanuts?"

-Orville to Wilbur

"It's the new world! I have discovered the new world! I've done it!... Wait, who are those people on the beach?"

-Columbus

"Tale of Ten Cities is too much, babe. Maybe two, tops!"

-Dickens' editor

"Carlos, you drivin'? Good. Juan, did you bring your van?"

-Santa Ana working out
transportation to the Alamo

"Oh no, not another whale! Boy, the tuna business is the pits."

-Captain Ahab's first job

"Let me see. Sneak 40 slaves from Cumberland across state line. Make contact with Martinsville hideout. Soak collards."

-Harriet Tubman going over her
To Do list

"Yo, Columbus. Dude, we're out of cheese, man!"

-*The First Mate*

"You're not going to believe this! I'm sitting on my front porch swing on a beautiful day. A flock of geese is flying over. Next thing I know, one of these geese dies in mid-air, falls out of the sky and hits me on the head. I was knocked unconscious. Have you ever been hit in the head by a dead 25 pound goose traveling about 85 mph?"

-*Methuselah in a letter*

"Listen you little smart ass. I made you what you are. When I say get me some coffee, then get me some coffee!"

-P. T. Barnum to Tom Thumb

"Hold on son, that's not how you turn a mouse into a newt!"

-Merlin's father

"Enough with the play dough. How about Mr. Potato Head for your birthday?"

-Rodin's mother

"Let me see. Snort a line of cocaine. Finish bottle of whiskey. Finish writing The Raven. Marry 13 year old cousin."

-Edgar Allen Poe going over his
To Do list

"That's right, and then you lay another thin strip of pig next to that one."

-*Sir Francis Bacon*

"Well! How many people have you murdered today?"
-*Mrs. Stalin*

"What was I thinking? Why did I bring two lice with us?"
-*Noah*

"Dear, why all this talk about riding a beam of light?"
-*Einstein's mother*

"When in doubt, be arrogant!"
-*French proverb*

"I'm feeling a little chunky.   I'm thinking about ordering that thighmaster."

-President Taft

"I still can't believe we sold them Alaska!"

-Boris Yeltsin

"Rub some more oil on your bones, hon?"

-Girl on the beach where Death takes a holiday

"Excuse me Mrs. Jensen, but for some reason I have a real problem with creationism."

-Charles Darwin in eighth grade science class

"Get your ape hands off me!"

-A drunk Charles Darwin

"He's not very good with people, but he loves numbers!"

-Archimedes' mother

"Honey, what do you say we make some peanut butter and jelly sandwiches, fly to Wright Patterson Air Force Base, and look at the dead alien bodies?"

-Jimmy Carter to Rosalyn

"Clear the passage to this exit or I'll shut you down."

-John Paul Sartre in his previous
life as a fire inspector

"Hey P.A., do that impression of Uncle Toulouse again!"

-Mrs. Renoir, to young Pierre August Renoir,
one of the founders of modern Impressionism,
who quit painting in 1882, moved to the
Catskills, and became a prop comic

"Hey mom, how do you draw a pig?"

-*young Rembrandt*

"The cards keep coming up negative on the Brutus guy."

-*Caesar's psychic*

"That better be a dove with a twig in it's mouth, because if I see another vulture...."

-*Noah on deck the 40th day*

"Now let me see, was that a green seed or a yellow seed that I planted there? I can't remember! Oh well, I'll just mark down a yellow seed."

-*Gregor Mendel documenting his 8 year plant experiments*

"Butter, a sprinkle of salt, a little basil, and they're not bad."

-Gregor Mendel conversing with a delegate at the local pea festival

"Honey, we're just going to see the Kennedys drive by. Do we have to take this stupid movie camera?"

-Mr. Zapruder to his wife

"Hey, who's that guy on the grassy knoll?"

-JFK

"Clyde, is everything set in Dallas today to assassinate the President?   Good.   Our men are in place to triangulate in Dealy Plaza? Good. And Oswald is set up to take the fall? Good. Oh, did you find that floral print mu-mu for me?   You know, the one with the pretty pink bows? Okay."

-J. Edgar Hoover on the phone with Clyde Tolson on the morning of November 22, 1963

"Hey, shut up, I'm talking!"

-Socrates during a speech

"Man inherently has a universal... hey, who spilt coffee on my toga?"

-Plato during a speech

"Hey Ben, have you seen my kite?"

-Ben Franklin's neighbor

"Okay men, before we go pillage and plunder, please remember where we parked the boat."

-Leif Ericsson

"Men, I'm going to have to put my foot down.
No more coffee breaks. We're Vikings!"

-Leif Ericsson

"I'm sick of hearing about light bulbs. We need food on this table."

-Mrs. Edison

"I'm sorry Karl. We can't print your book. The Typesetters' Union is on strike."

-Karl Marx's publisher

"What is it about these Mongol hordes that makes them so damned ornery?"

-The Emperor Han

"Hey Socrates, when are you going to get a job?"

-Socrates' neighbor

"How can we call this a settlement when we're about two days away from starving to death and the Indians could kill us at any moment?"

-*A nervous, stressed out settler at Jamestown*

"Honey, get out the serum. One of the rattlers bit me again."

-*Noah on the Ark*

"If a fly lands on your head, never try to kill it with a ball peen hammer."

-*Bulgarian proverb*

"You'll never be as famous as Columbus."

-*Vasco da Gama's mother*

"Scurvy, schmurvy, don't let it get the best of you, men!"

-Vasco da Gama dealing with disease and low morale on his ship

"Actually, when I look out over a field and see my legions of Romans clash against thousands of Brits, I like a nice light back rub."

"Jane, I've noticed you like to date really hairy men."

"Good Lord, how can I tell these people we worship burnt shrubbery?"

"Hey Socrates, they're hiring for the late-night shift down at the plant. They let you talk at night, while you work. You'd like that!"

"Can somebody get those hyenas, roosters, parrots, wolves, and wild boar to shut up! I'm trying to get some sleep."

-Noah on the Ark

"Well, have you had their mint juleps? They're great!"

-Ulysses S. Grant on reasons for attacking the South

"General, I must insist you say 'Uncle!'"

-Grant to Lee at Appomattox

"I liked the name Crazy Horse. Your dad wanted to name you Insane Mule."

-Crazy Horse's mother

"Oooooooooh, oooooooooooooooh, I've got a
cramp in my leg."

-*Sitting Bull*

"...then I fell off the roof and cracked my head wide open. I don't know what possessed me to say to the neighborhood kids 'your ball is on the roof, I'll get it.' At 726 years of age I should just burn the house down before I climb on it. To top it off, on the way to the doctor's office, I had kidney failure and an epileptic attack, my 12th in 150 years. I had to sit for two hours to see Dr. Lyman. Here I am bleeding with a split skull, kidney failure, and the residue of an epileptic attack, plus, on the way in some snot-nosed kid slammed the door on my finger. The doctor saw 4 kids with colds before he saw me. When I went up to the nurse's window, practically holding my brains in my hands, the nurse had the gall to look at me and go 'Oh, Methuselah, you again!'"

-Methuselah in a letter

"Why don't you apply for a job in the circus?"

-*Tom Thumb's neighbor*

"I still don't understand how you can build a railroad underground!"

-*Harriet Tubman's neighbor*

"Hey Moses! I haven't seen you in forty years. Where have you been?"

-*Moses' neighbor*

"Honey, what do you say we fly out to Wright Patterson Air Force Base, catch Happy Hour, and then go look at the dead alien bodies?"

-*President Gerald Ford to Betty*

"Hey Nostradamus, you still havin' those weird dreams?"

-*Nostradamus' neighbor*

"A year ago he's just General Alexander. Now he's Alexander the Great, and he hardly speaks to us anymore."

-A soldier in Alexander the Great's army

"When I say put your pencils down, I mean put your pencils down."

-Plato in front of his class
at the end of a test

"Excuse me sir, it's the Magna Carta, not the Magnetic Charter."

-An aide interrupting Cromwell
during a speech

"Hey, does anybody have an extension cord?"

-Edison after finding the correct filament

"I had a sphinx once for a pet! Nasty animal."
                                    -Early Egyptian craftsman

"Honey, where'd our couch go?"
                                              -Mrs. Freud

"Somebody contact the Gideons."
                    -Guttenberg after printing his first Bible

"Love is never having to say 'Get out or I'll have you killed.'"
                                              -Genghis Khan

"Okay, let's say for instance, one of the elephants falls overboard. Should we go ahead and throw the other elephant overboard?"

-Noah quizzing his crew

"You're not going to believe what's going on. First, before I get into it, I want to buy a male and female of every animal you have, except those nasty aardvarks. They can drown for all I care. Anyway, I know you're an atheist, but God has spoken to me. He says that the world will flood real soon and that I'm supposed to build an ark, which is much bigger than our canoe we built last year. I'm supposed to get two of every animal. I keep forgetting to ask him about insects. Then the world will flood for forty days and forty nights. How I'm supposed to feed all these animals for forty days and nights is beyond me. Some animals may become extinct because I'll have to feed them to other animals. My other problem is that I can only tell so many people because everybody is supposed to be killed in the flood. Everybody will want to get on my ark. Then again, what if it doesn't flood at all, and I've got this big ark sitting in my front yard with tons of animals. I guess I'll either start a zoo or have a big barbecue. Write me!"

-Noah in a letter

"Excuse me John Paul. I believe the correct phrasing is 'God and I', not 'me and God'!"

-Cardinal Spadini interrupting
the Pope during Mass

"If one more person asks me, 'When are we going to fight the Persians? When are we going to fight the Persians?', then we are not going to fight the Persians!"

-Alexander the Great

"When in doubt about the correct word or phrase, slur with a heavy accent."

-Scottish proverb

"Honey, can we go see the dead alien bodies again? Can we? Huh? Can we?"

-Dan Quayle to his wife, Marilyn

"I know there's a bug on me! Just leave it alone!"

-Mahavira (599 BC - 527 BC),
founder of Jainism whose beliefs
include not killing anything,
even an insect crawling on your
body, even if it bites you

"Dude, I think you're taking this monk thing a little too seriously!"

-A friend of Mahavira's who saw
him years later when he was a
monk and had shed all
materialism, even to the point of
walking naked in the streets

"Men, if we take Saltillo, fajitas for everybody!"

-General Zachary Taylor motivating
his troops before he took Saltillo,
Mexico, during the Mexican war

"Okay, which do you like the best? 'A house divided cannot stand', or 'a house divided is a duplex'?"

-Lincoln talking to his writers

"Heads, I fight for the South, tails, I fight for the North."

-General Lee flipping a coin to
decide his allegiance

"My God, all the men sure are spending a lot of time in the bathroom!"

-Cortez making an observation the day
after killing Montezuma

"Oh boy, another snorkel. Thanks, Dad."

-Philippe, son of Jacques Cousteau,
opening a birthday present

"Actually, I don't mind cereal without milk."
-*Louis Pasteur's neighbor*

"Pottsdam is too damn cold this time of year. Tell Uncle Joe we'll meet him in the Bahamas."
-*Harry Truman*

"Do we have to do that ping pong ball thing again?"
-*Captain Kangaroo*

"Is this thing on? Testing... 1... 2... 3... is it on? I can't tell! Who's back there? *IS IT ON?* Okay, that's it. The sound guy is going to Hell if I have anything to do with it! He'll never work in Vatican City again!"
-*the Pope doing a sound check*

"Dear, how much longer are you going to be on the phone?"

-Alexander Graham Bell to his wife

"Dick Morris is on the phone! Is the hooker listening?"

-President Clinton

"Let me see. Smoke a joint. Write. Smoke a joint. Eat. Smoke a joint. Get to gig."

-Bob Dylan going over his
To Do list

"I don't like it there! Move it!"

-Cheops when he saw the
finished pyramid

"What purpose can this serve except to be a non-functional physical tribute to oppression of the masses through hard labor?"

-Two slaves discussing the pyramids

"...and it rained so hard, the roof collapsed on me and I was trapped for three days. Sam, I thought this was it. Here I was at 802 years of age. I've had more physical ailments and tragedies than anyone in history. At the end of the third day, I was ready. I could almost see the white light. I really felt it was my time. Then a band of hooligans came over the hill, about 60 of them in all. They saved me, Sam. They pulled me out from under the rubble. I couldn't believe it. Then they set fire to everything and left. As I lay there in severe pain by my favorite oak tree, with my house collapsed and burned to a crisp, it started to rain. Then it started to pour, then thunder, then lightning struck the oak tree and it fell on me. It fell right on my knees. All I could think of was that I had just had reconstructive surgery. Got to go, my hand is cramping. Come by sometime!"

-**Methuselah in a letter**

"I panicked the other day. The ark is half built and it started to pour. I thought it was the big one. The neighbors said they've never seen me hammer so fast. Your skepticism is understood. All I can tell you is wait and see, just keep your canoe ready. Do you know where I can get some giraffes? Vinny the grocer said he's located two, but they are both males. That does me no good once the planet is washed clean. Have you ever tried to run down two giraffes and check their gender? I'm running full speed, am about to throw the rope and I pull a hamstring. I naturally pulled up, and when I hit the ground I cracked my shoulder on a big jagged rock. At that point, I was thinking that drowning might not be so bad. Why God ever made skunks is beyond me. The next flood, I'm going to wait and collect those little bastards last. The wife still won't let me sleep inside. I'm also thinking about collecting just two snakes, I don't care what kind they are. Next to rhinos, they are probably the biggest hassle. I've caught three rhinos and I've got to let one go, but everyone in the neighborhood won't let me. Rhinos are probably the hardest to keep fed and chained up. The one I call Lucy broke loose the other day and nearly destroyed the monkey cage. Thank God she didn't open a hole in the Gorilla pen. Anyway, I've got to go, plenty to do."

-*Noah in a letter*

"Albert, do you have any theories on why the relatives keep coming to visit?"

-Einstein's father

"It's really better that England owns the Falkland Islands."

-*Argentinean proverb*

"Ron, what do you say we fly out to Wright Patterson Air Force Base, look at the dead alien bodies, then go to dinner?"

-*Nancy Reagan*

"If you are skiing and run into an elk, just get up, apologize, and move on."

-*Norwegian proverb*

"If you are skiing and run into an elk, then kill it, skin it, and cook it!"

-*Russian proverb*

"Listen, it's really none of your business, but why don't you shoot that 'coon and skin it before you put it back on your head?"

-Doctor treating Davy Crockett
for minor bites and scratches

"You know what I love about conquering new territory? Having a cup of fresh coffee afterward and gazing over my newly acquired domain. I feel such pride."

-Hannibal

"To me there is nothing more humorous than a Philistine with an arrow through his skull!"

-King David

"Sir, the men are calling you Mr. Fluffy Pants!"

-*The First Mate*

"Love is never having to say 'Would it be all right if I pulled that knife out of your back now?'"

-Kublai Khan

"Love is wine, flowers, and a sharpened 20 foot pole."

-Vlad the Impaler

"That's right, Zeus. I get it there by 10:30am the next day, or it's free."

-Mercury, messenger of the gods

"Let me see. Finish quart of gin, work on cigarette joke, have another quart of gin."

-W. C. Fields going over his To Do list

"So there I am riding through a band of angry heretics, when all of a sudden I get this burning, itching feeling."

-Sir Lancelot talking to this doctor

"In the name of God, St. George, and St. Michael, I knight thee... oh, I'm sorry, I seem to have cut your neck."

-King Richard knighting his first knight

"First we hit them with the archers to thin them out. Pass the toast. Then we hurl large rocks at them with our catapults. Pass the bacon, the plate with the crispy. Then we unleash our horsemen... where's the fruit? I don't see the fresh fruit! I'll hang the man responsible! BRING ME THE FRESH FRUIT NOW! Then we annihilate them with our infantry."

-William the Conqueror at brunch

"If you can't find the Grail, bring back some sandwiches!"

-King Arthur

"I think we should shorten it from Icecubeland to just Iceland."

-*Debate in the Icelandic Parliament over the naming of the country*

"All right then, I'll throw in two tickets to Disneyworld."

-*General Colin Powell convincing General Cedras to give up power in Haiti.*

"Let me see. March 110 miles. Destroy German army. Then meditation with aroma therapy."

-*General George S. Patton going over his To Do list*

"You know you've had too much wine when you are polite to Americans."

-French proverb

"These foreigners won't make it here!"

-Pocahontas' father

"I'm naming this land Virginia after Queen Elizabeth, the Virgin Queen. At least they say she's a virgin. My friend Eddie says he slept with her."

-Sir Walter Raleigh

"Who brought all this cranberry sauce?"

-Captain of the Mayflower

"Boy, wouldn't it suck if the Nazi's took France?"
-*Charles DeGaulle before WWII*

"Sonny, Red, get Dr. Nick on the phone. Tell him I need some more dilaudid, the green pills, and tell Cilla to fix me another fried peanut butter and banana sandwich, and if the dilaudid gets here in time, tell her to sprinkle a few on the fried peanut butter and banana sandwich."
-*Elvis*

"My cards show that Bush is actually not a wimp."
-*Noriega's psychic*

"I keep seeing pigs and water!"
-*Castro's psychic*

"P. T., I don't like the name Tom Thumb, I like the name Tony Gazelle. Why are you so stuck on Tom Thumb?"

-Tom Thumb discussing his
stage name with P. T. Barnum

"Love is all of my legions going into battle, triumph, and of course, my blankie."

-Alexander the Great

"Love is a breast, a thigh, a leg, and cole slaw."

-Colonel Sanders

"Tortoise soup again? Didn't we bring *any* provisions?"

-*Charles Darwin, one week in the Galapagos*

"Let me see. Pack for Chicago. Swing golf clubs. Kill Nicole."

-O. J. going over his
To Do list

"You'll give me how much for my pet chicken?"
*-Young Frank Purdue learns a valuable
lesson during the Great Depression*

"You're not going to light that, are you?"
-Joan of Arc

"Why did Hess buy a kilt?"
-Hitler going over his bills

"I think he's a bookie. Says he's into numbers."
-Descartes' neighbor

"Let's talk about something else besides math."

-A woman talking to Descartes at a bar

"...and just at that moment, my quintuple great nephew opened the bathroom door. It hit my hand and the Q-Tip went right through my eardrum. I fell backwards, screaming, and nearly broke my neck on the tub. Luckily, I only ruptured a vertebra. On the way to the doctor's office, one of the wheels slipped off the cart and I fell into the road. As I lay there, three carts ran over me. One was carrying stones. I suffered 14 broken bones and multiple contusions. Come by sometime!"

-Methuselah in a letter

"Why are we building pyramids when our social programs are so underfunded?"

-Early Egyptian Left-Wing Democrat

"Quit tapping on the table and say what you want to say!"

-Mrs. Samuel Morse

"When opening a Chinese restaurant, be sure to use small, cheap, inexpensive, plastic forks for take-out orders."

-Chinese proverb

"If you are tired of sitting, there must be an acquitting. No. If the jello jiggles, there must be an acquittal. No. If serving on a jury is the pits, you must acquit. No."

-Johnnie Cochran working on his closing statement

"Maybe you didn't hear me. I said, 'Red rover, red rover, send Fluffy Pants right over.'"

-*The First Mate*

"No, I disagree. I say it's Mercury, but the wife thinks that Venus is the center of the universe."

-Copernicus' neighbor

"Does the phrase 'Rope a dope' mean anything to you?"

-George Foreman's psychic before the fight in Zaire with Ali

"If you want a really good meal, go to France."

-English proverb

"What do you mean, you have not yet begun to rake your yard?"

-John Paul Jones' neighbor

"Listen, I hate to bother you, but can you look in your thesaurus and tell me another word for 'Curb your dog'?"

-Roget's neighbor

"Never play poker with a fortune cookie manufacturer."

-Chinese proverb

"I have no idea where I am!"

-*Amelia Earhart*

"We don't want to blow no more and knock down walls Josh. Me and the fellas want to form our own Jazz Trio."

-*Overheard at Jericho*

"Tastes like tap water to me."

-*Ponce de Leon testing a possible fountain of youth*

"If one's country is overrun, you can always call the Americans."

-*French proverb*

"Caesar had his Brutus, and Charles I had his Cromwell. All I have is a dog named Chester."

-*Young Patrick Henry*

"So McClellan wants to build a large wooden horse and hide our men inside, hoping the rebels will bring it into their camp."

-*Lincoln to Grant*

"I was thinking that after we defeat the Confederacy, we sell Florida to Brazil to pay for the war."

-*General McClellan*

"If a bear charges at you, close your eyes and pretend you are a piece of wood. Never pretend you are a slow-roasting chicken."

-*Russian proverb*

"Forgive me, Queen, but I don't like the names 'Nina', 'Pinta', and 'Santa Maria'. How about just Boat #1, Boat #2, and Boat #3?"

-Columbus talking to Queen Isabella

"When following a herd of buffalo, be careful where you step."

-Native American proverb

"Never play chicken with a train."

-Polish proverb

"A pastry a day will keep the doctor away."

-Danish proverb

"Why do you call it the Pythagorean Theorem, ... Jim?"

-Pythagoras' neighbor

"Jacques, will you please quit narrating what the fish are doing in the aquarium and eat your dinner."

-Jacques Cousteau's mother

"You know, I think we made a big mistake!"

-Goering whispering to Hess during the Nuremberg trials

"If a gorilla is charging you, close your eyes and pretend you are a stone. Never pretend you are a small jungle creature."

-Tanzanian proverb

"Flank, flank, flank, that's all I ever hear from you people. I need new ideas."

-Caesar discussing strategy with his generals

"Land ha! I mean Land ho!"

-Columbus

"...and the picnic layout was beautiful. We were just about to have lunch when all of a sudden, a plague of locusts came over the hill. They covered the horizon. I'm 862 years old and have seen just about everything, but this was a first. They make a humming noise that gets increasingly deafening. I actually wasn't fearful as much as I was curious. They looked like a large dark blanket coming at us. As they got closer, I tried to count them, but that was useless. I stopped at sixteen. The weird thing about a plague of locusts is that right before they get up on you they look rather friendly. You can see their eyes. But once they get to you it's like hitting a brick wall. They knocked me back so hard, my head went into the potato salad bowl and squashed every bit of potato salad out of the bowl. I recovered, but I'm still finding locusts hither and yon."

-Methuselah in a letter

"So what was my great great great great great great grandfather like?"

"So what are you telling me, my great grandfather was a gorilla?"

-Darwin's neighbor

"Hey Noah, I hear you're starting a zoo!"

-Noah's neighbor

"Never go swimming while holding a bunch of bricks."

-Manitoban proverb

"Now, is it 'i' before 'e' except after 'c', or 'd'?"

-young Noah Webster

"Never be on the same team with someone named Hitler."

-Italian proverb

"If you see a leprechaun riding the Loch Ness monster, go home."

-Irish proverb

"Never stick your hand in a light socket."

-Manitoban proverb

"When building a teepee, always follow the directions."

-Native American proverb

"I had a dream last night that has been a fear of mine lately. It's about the future state of Alaska. I know Mr. Seward is negotiating the purchase from the Russians. If it happens I fear they will join the South, swoop down through Canada, and surprise the Union forces. This epic move would swing the tide towards the Confederacy. I look forward to your opinion."

-General McClellan in a letter to President Lincoln

"You are relieved of your duties as Commander of the Union forces. I've decided to appoint you to the Park Rangers post in Anchorage, Alaska."

-Lincoln in a letter to General McClellan

"He's gonna make the Red Sea part!"
"Moses? The same guy with the burning bush story?"

-*Two Hebrews*

"McClellan wrote me from Alaska saying he's afraid that Brazil will join the Confederacy, swoop around the east coast, and take Staten Island. Now, don't get me wrong. I like bourbon as much as the next guy, but I don't think Brazil can swoop."

-Ulysses S. Grant in a letter to Lincoln

"I just received the oddest correspondence from ex-General McClellan of the Union forces saying he thought Mozambique was interested in taking our side. He said he had communicated with their president, and that we should look into the matter promptly for this would swing to tide of war in favor of the Confederacy. He said he thought that the Mozambique forces could swoop around the Cape of Good Hope, then swoop into Pennsylvania behind Union forces. He suggested that you and I, and all the major players in the Confederacy, go to Mozambique at once to discuss the matter. First, what is McClellan doing in Alaska? Second, can Mozambique actually swoop?"

-General Robert E. Lee in a letter
to Jefferson Davis

"How many times do I have to tell you? Stay away from those train tracks!"

-Doppler's mother

"When hammering a nail, never put your thumb on the head of the nail."

-Manitoban proverb

"When catching your neighbor's cat for dinner, entice him with dried cat food."

-North Korean proverb

"If you don't like sushi, cook it."

-Japanese proverb

"Shut up, Oliver! You'll never rule England! Now eat your peas."

-Oliver Cromwell's father

"I see now the brilliance of your move. Historically speaking, putting me here in Anchorage was masterful. You realized my purpose before I did, and I appreciate your confidence. I now understand my role in the North's effort to defeat the South. I am the 'think-tank' and the 'disinformer.' I have just this past week sent a letter to General Lee saying that Mozambique was highly interested in supporting the Confederate cause. The key was suggesting that he, Davis, and all the major players in the South go to Mozambique ASAP to work out the details. While they are gone, the North will swoop into the South and end the war. Thank you again for your support."

-*General McClellan in a letter to Lincoln*

"You want to come join in the Hokey Pokey?"

-*The First Mate*

"When hungry, cold, and out of vodka, revolt!"

-Russian proverb

"When killing someone in the name of Allah, always slash the sword from right to left."

-Iranian proverb

"When killing someone in the name of Allah, always slash the sword from left to right."

-Iraqi proverb

"Never invite a cow to your family reunion unless you are absolutely sure it is a reincarnated relative."

-East Indian proverb

"One atomic bomb is plenty."

"When a polar bear charges at you, close your eyes and pretend you are a snowball, not a small baby seal."

"Darn it! My chapstick broke and melted all in my purse! And I have to get off to that Nobel prize banquet!"

"Again, oh my Lord, you shouldn't have!"

-Madame Curie when she found out she won her second Nobel prize for radium research

"Always be careful not to wave chopsticks around in the air, because you could poke somebody's eye out."
-Chinese proverb

"Never punch a cop."
-Manitoban proverb

"There is nothing so dear.... We have nothing to cheer... uh, no. Nothing to spear. No... to jeer, steer... Eleanor! Bring me a beer! ...Nothing to steer, it will steer itself. Oh boy, I fear the worst."
-F.D.R. working out the kinks in his first inaugural address

"...and I cut my little toe clean off. You wouldn't think that could happen with a pedicure."

-Methuselah in a letter

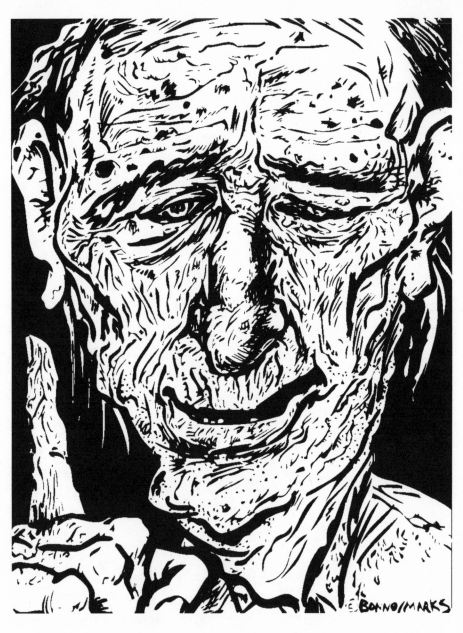

"You're as young as you feel!"

-Methuselah, the day before he died

"Let me see. Call Mom. Screw investors. Donate a little cash to a charity."

-*Ivan Boesky going over his*
To Do list

"I keep seeing mice."

-*Young Walt Disney's psychic*

"Let me see. Write 2 pages of material. Organize notes. Shoot heroine. Get to gig."

-*Lenny Bruce going over his*
To Do list

"What do you mean you don't have any toys? You have billions and billions of toys!"

-*Mrs. Sagan to young Carl*

"Never threaten the United States."

"When frostbite starts to set in, quit making love."

"Never smoke after three plates of refried beans."

"Boy, wouldn't it suck if Sherman burned Atlanta?"

"How long 'til we get to the new world? Five minutes less than the last time you asked me."

-Leif Ericsson

"...so after my 300th heart attack, my kids threw me a party. Just my luck, as I'm blowing out the candles, I have my 301st heart attack. I'm so used to them now. People ask me how I've withstood over 300 heart attacks. I tell them the truth. I make heart attacks my friend."

-Methuselah in a letter

"Traveling at the speed of light is okay, as long as you're home for dinner."

-*Einstein's mother*

"I keep telling them plaid is in, but they keep saying they want stars and stripes."

-*Betsy Ross*

"War and Peace and a Cat Named Kalamazoo. Leo, I think we need some focus here."

-*Tolstoy's editor*

"Hey tonight, snow ice cream is on me!"

-*Rear Admiral Peary coming back from the North Pole*

"Man, I'm still freezing my butt off!"

-Rear Admiral Peary coming back from the North Pole

"Boy, wouldn't it suck if there were thousands of Indians over that hill!"

-*Custer*

"Son, I've told you a hundred times. Don't pet the Boa Constrictors."

-*Mrs. Noah*

"Boy, wouldn't it suck if the peasants revolted and killed our entire family by firing squad?"

-*Czar Nicholas*

"Never jump out of a car traveling 100 miles per hour down hill!"

-*Manitoban proverb*

"I wish I had a drachma for every Ottoman I killed with a right sword slash to the neck."

-Alexander the Great

"Let me see. Take the Alamo. Kill remaining survivors. Two hours of yoga and meditation. Eat big plate of refried beans with extra Monterrey Jack cheese."

-Santa Ana going over his
To Do list

"Okay, here are the votes. Turkey, 110; Chicken, 18; Fowl, 12. Turkey wins, the name of our country is Turkey."

-Turkish Parliament

"Zip-a-de-do-dah, zip-a-de-ay! My, oh my, what a wonderful day! Plenty of sunshine headin' my way! Zip-a-de-do-dah, zip-a-de-... hey, where's my compass?"

-Amelia Earhart

"If I only had a nickel for every Turk I impaled."
                                                   -Vlad the Impaler

"Honey, what do you say we fly to Wright Patterson Air Force Base, have some barbecue, then go poke the dead alien bodies with cattle prods?"
                                  -President Lyndon Johnson
                                           to Lady Bird

"Never try to swallow a toothpick sideways!"
                                           -Manitoban proverb

"Hey, cancel the hemlock. How about just a frozen pina colada?"

-*Socrates*

"Did you go to Florida?"

-*Columbus' neighbor*

"Let me see. Wake up. Walk 2 miles. Eat a small oak tree."

-*Euell Gibbons going over his*
To Do list

"Dick, I am not a drunk!"

-*Pat Nixon*

"So these two Indians walk into a bar and
they've both got on these really fluffy pants..."

-*The First Mate*

160

BIOGRAPHICAL STUFF

CHRIS BONNO

Chris Bonno thinks John Marks is funny. He has laughed many times at 8:30 AM when Mr. Marks would call with a resounding "MR. BONNNOOO!" They have also done numerous improv shows together in Austin, TX, where they met. Bonno was born in Houston, TX, and now resides in Los Angeles, CA, where he pursues a career in magazine illustration, art, acting, improv, and comedy. He has appeared on *Married with Children, Mad About You,* and *The Naked Truth.* His artwork has appeared on *Caroline in the City, The LA Weekly,* and in *National Lampoon* magazine where Lost Quotes made its first appearance in 1994. A major achievement is in your hands, a collection of his drawings in a book that he can show his mother at the nearest bookstore.

MAURY HARRIS

Maury Harris, a writer living in Philadelphia, PA, was born in the house his father built, physically, in Jackson, MS. After graduating from LSU, he set his sights on becoming a secretary in a small welding firm, a goal he has yet to realize.

John Marks has made Maury laugh since the age of two.

SO, YOU GOT A KICK OUT OF THE BOOK?

NOW and only now...

HAN HOUSE PUBLISHING

Established Recently

By decree of Prince Chan, a direct descendant of Emperor Han, living in exile since the cultural revolution, **PRESENTS:**

LOST QUOTES on T-SHIRTS

Yes, you can now own any of the cartoon quotes in the book on a 100% heavy weight, parchment*dyed cotton T-Shirt with dark screened print.

CHOOSE FROM THE FOLLOWING 52, COUNT 'EM, 52 ITEMS!

§ THE FINE PRINT: Cover Van Gogh VANCO is only available in full color as shown on cover, on a parchment dyed T-Shirt (see cover parchment). Yes, it looks great, but it is also more money! See next page for more details. * Not real parchment. No animals were harmed or mistreated during this process. It's more of a "mountain wash".

IF YOU FOLLOW THESE INSTRUCTIONS, WE WILL ACTUALLY SEND YOU A SHIRT!

If you order: **Darwin Style #DAR71**, this is how your shirt will look.

"Get your ape hands off me!"

-A drunk Charles Darwin

Send **$12.00 * +
$3.00 S & H to:**
(Check or Money Order)

**Han House
Publishing
P.O. Box 511
Bryn Athyn, PA
19009
Hey! Order Guy**

**Include:
Title, Style #
Size: L, XL, or XXL
How Many?
Return Address**

Pennsylvania Residents add
6% Sales Tax

PLEASE MAKE CHECKS OR
MONEY ORDERS PAYABLE TO:

Han House Publishing

Please allow 6-8 weeks
for delivery.

*MORE FINE PRINT:
Van Gogh VANCO is priced
at $15.00 + S&H and sales
tax if applicable. Color
costs more!

**IF YOU INCLUDE AN EXTRA $1.50 WITH YOUR ORDER,
WE WILL INCLUDE IN YOUR SHIPMENT, THE CURRENT
ISSUE OF *HordeWatch* (A $2.50 VALUE).**

SEE NEXT PAGE FOR DETAILS.

HAN HOUSE
P U B L I S H I N G ®

Established Recently

In keeping with our promise:
NEVER AGAIN, TO LET
MONGOL HORDES SWEEP
DOWN FROM THE STEPPES
AND RUIN EVERYTHING...

Is Proud to Present:

Volume 1
1997

$2.50

HordeWatch

A Han House
Publication

OUR PLEDGE   **WORRY NOT, WE ARE WATCHING!**   **TO YOU**

Still No Sign of 'em

By Simon Marks
ASSOCIATED PRESS

Wan Su Province— "So far in this year of 1997 we ain't seen hide nor hair of them roudy folks", says Little Richard Toenail, Chief Investigating Officer with the Horde Patrol. an ever vigilant arm of the local police department.

"I guess it was about 1400 years ago that these vicious devils burst onto the local scene", Toenail added. Our records actually put that burst at 1600 years ago. An authority on the subject. Toenail is well known and even better respected for his opinions. If Toenail says he "ain't seen nuthin'", then that's good enough for the folks around these parts.

PHOTO BY "MONTAGE" JOE

Hordes Not Really So Bad

By Mandy Wade
BIT MAGAZINE

Sheeder Mill. PA— K. P. Swenson. a local horse trainer and trail guide has recently published an article in the forthcoming August '97 *Hordes Illustrated* entitled. "Hordes Can Bite Me". In it. Swenson makes the claim that the Mongol hordes that swept down from the steppes centuries ago to pillage. burn and plunder were not all that threatening.

"Hell, they rode ponies. much like you would find in the kiddie rides at your local carnival. Granted. ponies are a bitch to ride, but you can swing up on 'em like you're steppin' over a pregnant sow. Now, how imposing is that? In comparison, you'd need a step-ladder to get up on your average thoroughbred.

They must have looked like a herd of young'uns. I mean. just add balloons and bingo. it's another damn birthday party. The fact that history paints these roving bands of barbarians as deadly and ruinous is Hollywood hogwash."

Swenson. a horse-woman from Yahoo County. adds. "If you want to get technical about it. picture Mickey Rooney on a Great Dane. There's your Mongol hordes." When asked about all of the death and destruction normally associated with the Mongols, Swenson states, "Sure. sure. attribute it to short-man's-complex. After all, if you give freedom and weapons to toddlers. you can expect trouble with a capital T."

CHINESE WEATHER FORECAST

Expect the worst, prepare for it, and it will happen.
If it doesn't. you look like damn fool.

Emperor Han's Pleasing Positions

By Dr. Jack Harris
HAN HOUSE PRESS

San Chi— A local woman here, who wishes to remain unnamed — as she was born without a name, has never needed one and says she has been doing just-fine-thank-you-very- much without one —. claiming to be a direct descendant of a once loved and heavily used concubine of the late. great Emperor Han. says that his secret to pleasing thousands of women during his long reign is about to be published.

The woman whose ancestor passed down the good sexual positions. has informed the local authorities that an American publishing house. which wishes to remain nameless as of this date. has offered her an unprecedented and undisclosed amount of money. to reveal the Emperors secrets. The woman has received an advance on the money to keep quiet until the book goes to print. When I offered her money to give me just one of the pleasing positions to print in this story she said. "OK". The position, known as the *twisted goose*, has apparently been enjoyed by the woman's family members for almost two thousand years. In order to enact "the goose", one partner must lay face down atop a small pool of water, while the other swims below him making continuous dives in an attempt to capture the sexual organs of the floating partner with a small wet made of goose down. Breathing is optional. and once the organs are "captured" the act is over.

When the woman was asked if she had partaken in this particular act, she replied, "Yes. many times." She was then asked to describe the sensation she had experienced. and she said. "It feels good."

The book. as yet untitled. is scheduled to hit bookstands in late 1999.

Steppes Not That Steep

By Dr. David Daniel
U.S. GEOLOGICAL SURVEY

Near the Gobi Desert— I have been searching for these so called steppes that supposed Mongol hordes rode down from centuries ago. for months and all I have found is this vast semi-arid plain. native to the area. I have also challenged the local authorities to show me any piece of landscape that might resemble a steppe, hill. hillock or even the slightest rise in elevation. as say a large rock might provide. Their response has been negatory so far.

Show me a small increase in elevation. or a tiny outcropping of independant geological means and we will have our proof. As long as none of the above continue to hide themselves from me. then there is no more a reason to continue this search, than looking for a pot of gold at the end of a rainbow.

Actually. a rainbow in this God forsaken desert might be the next project for me to get involved in.

That's one small steppe for a man, one giant leap for Mongol history.

Han's Brother's Tomb Found

By Jelly Bean Miles
TORANAGA PRESS

See Ping— A local plumbing contractor digging in the area of the Winter Palace here. has uncovered a shallow hole believed to be the lost tomb of Chin Les. estranged brother of Emperor Han. The tomb. sought after for centuries by Chinese historians is thought to contain the secret of turning gold into dung.

Legend states that Chin Les was exiled after bankrupting Han in a practical joke. If I were you. I'd cash in your yuan. now.

Q & A TIME WITH HHP'S Ph.D.

Q: What is a horde?
—R. Elson Tupac, VA
A: Webster defines this as a "throng or swarm". Much like you'd see at a Joni Mitchell concert.
Q: Is Joni Mitchell still performing? -M. Morris Arkansas City, KS
A: Yes. At small halls and benefits in Canada.
Q: Do Canadians still harbor ill feelings toward us Americans?
-H. Metzenbaum It, MS
A: About as ill as a Manitoban hangover.

Questions for Mr. Hametin? Write: Mr. H. C/O HHP P.O. Box 511 Bryn Athyn, PA 19009

If you find any:

LOST QUOTES

or have any questions or concerns about this book, please write us at:

Han House Publishing
P.O. Box 511
Bryn Athyn, PA 19009
Attn: Inquiries

Operators are not standing by to take your call, but people with letter openers are waiting to see what you have written.

Researching and finding Lost Quotes is a continual, lifelong project that has been bestowed on me. I find great satisfaction in this work. So stick around! It will be a great ride!

-John Marks

Upcoming Han House books:

- Lost Letters
- Lost Quotes, Volume 47
- The Dow De Cha-ching (Wall St. meets the Tao)
- Lost Diaries
- Lost References
- Lost Post-it™ Notes
- Lost Ideas
- Lost Art (Lost Sculptures)
- Lost Philosophies
- Lost Invoices
- Lost Photos
- Gift Ideas for Tyrants and Dictators
- Lost Book Titles
- Lost Crossword Puzzles
- Lost Poems, Haikus, Sonnets, and Limericks
- Kings, Queens, Peasants, and Parcheesi